This Books Belongs To.........

....

....

....

Trace the steps for making the letter a on the following line.

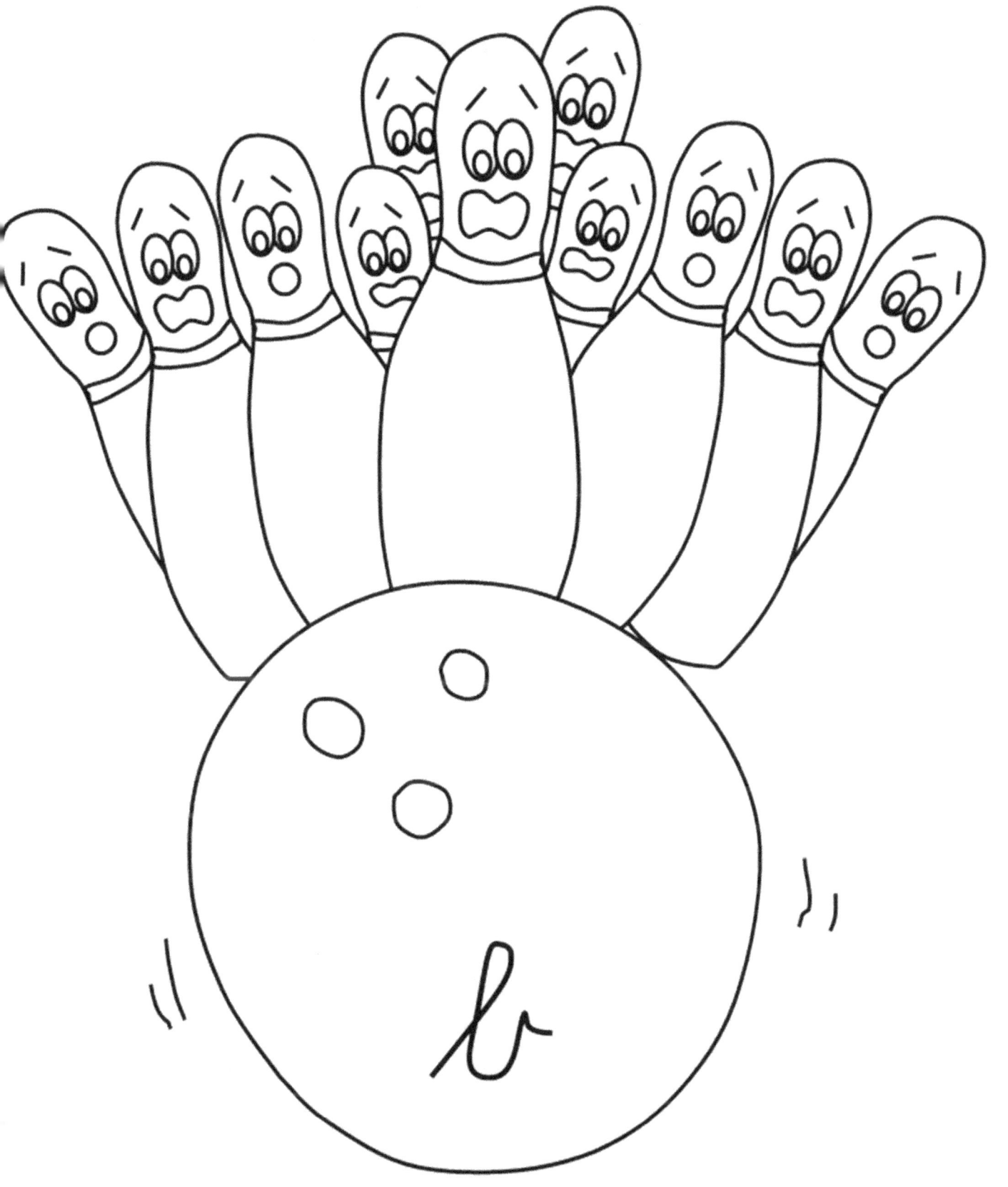

Trace the steps for making the letter b on the following line.

Trace the steps for making the letter c on the following line.

Trace the steps for making the letter c on the following line.

_c_ _h_ _ch_ _ch_ _ch_ _ch_

Trace the steps for making the letter d on the following line.

Trace the steps for making the letter e on the following line.

Trace the steps for making the letter f on the following line.

Trace the steps for making the letter g on the following line.

Trace the steps for making the letter h on the following line.

Trace the steps for making the letter i on the following line.

Trace the steps for making the letter j on the following line.

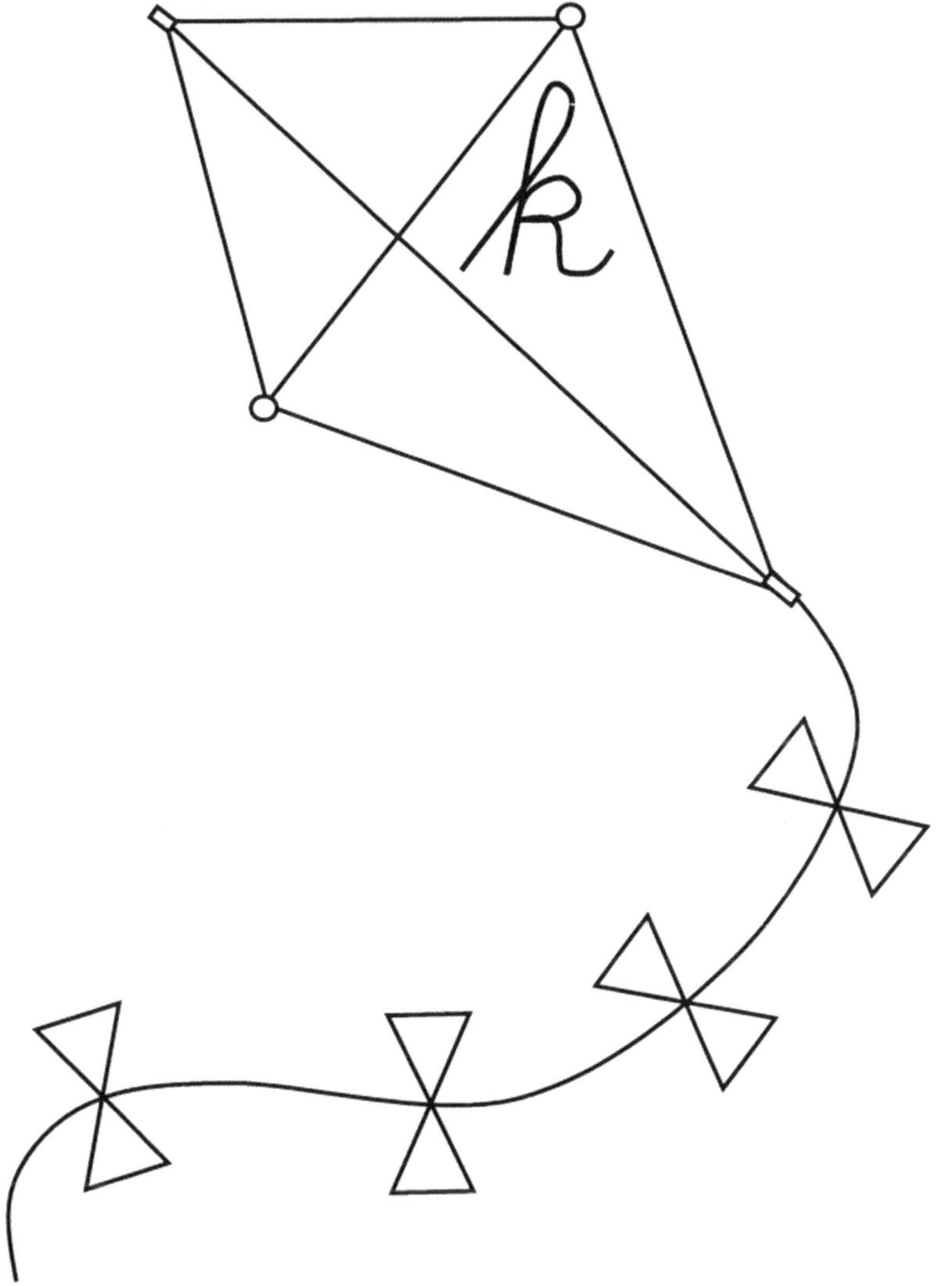

Trace the steps for making the letter k on the following line.

Trace the steps for making the letter l on the following line.

Trace the steps for making the letter m on the following line.

Trace the steps for making the letter n on the following line.

_n_ _n_ _n_ _n_ _n_ _n_ _n_ _n_ _nn_

Trace the steps for making the letter o on the following line.

Trace the steps for making the letter p on the following line.

Trace the steps for making the letter q on the following line.

$\mathcal{I} \quad \mathcal{I} \quad \mathcal{O} \quad \mathcal{Q} \quad \mathcal{Q} \quad \mathcal{Q} \quad \mathcal{Q}$

Trace the steps for making the letter r on the following line.

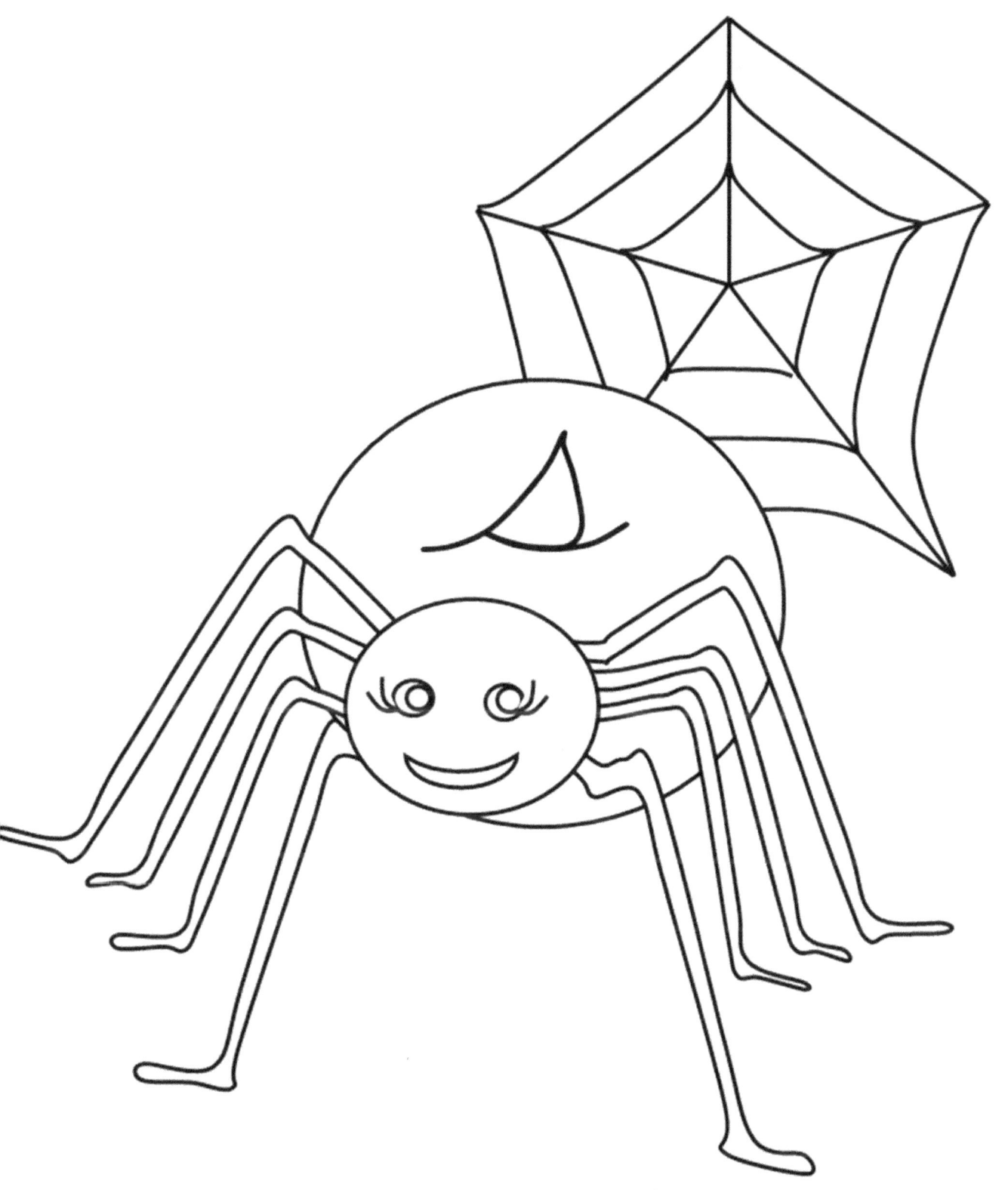

Trace the steps for making the letter s on the following line.

Trace the steps for making the letter sh on the following line.

sh   sh   sh   sh   sh

Trace the steps for making the letter t on the following line.

Trace the steps for making the letter th on the following line.

_t_ _h_ _th_ _th_ _th_ _th_

Trace the steps for making the letter u on the following line.

Trace the steps for making the letter v on the following line.

Trace the steps for making the letter w on the following line.

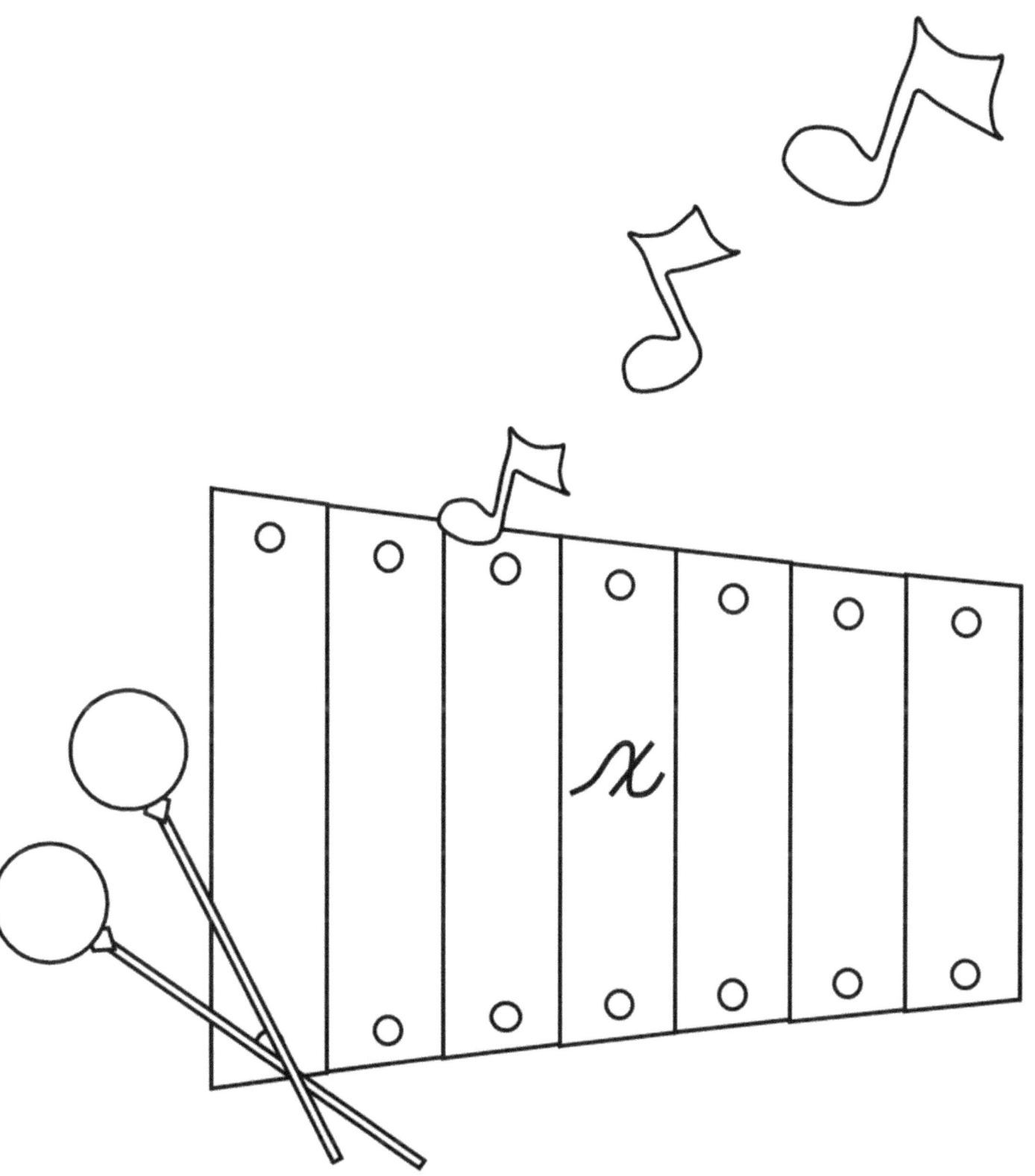

Trace the steps for making the letter x on the following line.

Trace the steps for making the letter y on the following line.

Trace the steps for making the letter z on the following line.

www.ingramcontent.com/pod-product-compliance
Lightning Source LLC
Chambersburg PA
CBHW081511220526
45467CB00010B/2871